About the Author

Laura Owen-Onsea is a first-time mum, a manager at work and a full-time wife. A British-born Canadian, she currently lives in the quiet suburbs of Antwerp, Belgium, with her husband and daughter, Stella. An engagement and relationship-building expert by profession, she set her mind to poetry whilst on maternity leave with her firstborn and hasn't looked back. Poetry, for her, combines all of the beauty and inspiration that lies around us, from our professional to personal life and gives us the opportunity to create what we are meant to create. Because inside all of us is a creator.

Around the Year in 365 Haikus

Laura Owen-Onsea

Around the Year in 365 Haikus

Olympia Publishers
London

www.olympiapublishers.com
OLYMPIA PAPERBACK EDITION

Copyright © Laura Owen-Onsea 2023

The right of Laura Owen-Onsea to be identified as author of
this work has been asserted in accordance with sections 77 and 78 of
the Copyright, Designs and Patents Act 1988.

All Rights Reserved

No reproduction, copy or transmission of this publication
may be made without written permission.
No paragraph of this publication may be reproduced,
copied or transmitted save with the written permission of the publisher,
or in accordance with the provisions
of the Copyright Act 1956 (as amended).

Any person who commits any unauthorised act in relation to
this publication may be liable to criminal
prosecution and civil claims for damage.

A CIP catalogue record for this title is
available from the British Library.

ISBN: 978-1-80439-002-3

This is a work of fiction.
Names, characters, places and incidents originate from the writer's
imagination. Any resemblance to actual persons, living or dead, is
purely coincidental.

First Published in 2023

Olympia Publishers
Tallis House
2 Tallis Street
London
EC4Y 0AB

Printed in Great Britain

Dedication

I dedicate this, my first book, to my first-born daughter, Stella. Always my inspiration, she has grown with me on this journey just like my writing has.

Acknowledgements

Writing this book came as a surprise to many as it started off as an extremely personal project that I wasn't sure I wanted to share with the world. But one person told me that I had to tell my story. So, my first thank you has to be to my husband and best friend, Bart. Thank you for believing in me, for encouraging me to keep writing and for convincing me to share my story. I will never forget the countless evenings we had on our sofa counting syllables out loud on our fingers – only you could make this project so much fun. Thank you to Maxime for your trust and friendship. You have a passion for believing in others, and it is truly beautiful. Thank you to my wonderful group of friends, both in Belgium and the UK. Claudia, my ride or die, thank you for always lifting me up. You define female empowerment. Marie, Dan, Carys, and Clare, thank you for the years of friendship. To Emily for the dedication to proof-reading first drafts. To so many others, thank you for your support. You know who you are. Last but not least, thank you to my publisher Olympia for guiding my journey, for looking at first edits and most of all, for taking the leap of faith into an unknown author. You inspire me and many to create and write.

I hope that you see
The ugly and the pretty
When you read my work

Act 1

January

1 January

It is a new year
But you would never have guessed
This year is a test

2 January

My beautiful girl
Big blue eyes looking at me
And that one blonde curl

3 January

Social media
The mum-shaming is misplaced
Unsolicited.

4 January

Making this all up
"I took the road less travelled"
Me as a parent

5 January

Submersed in Van Gogh
Let the power of light move
The feelings inside

6 January

> The news affects me
> Puts my rhythm off centre
> Need to re-align

7 January

> A walk with a friend
> One, two, three, be there for me
> Four, five, we both strive

8 January

> Girls' night in tonight
> Feeling that mama-bond ache
> Papa is so great

9 January

> New daily peak deaths
> One second to catch my breath
> How do we keep on?

10 January

> Keep on carry on
> Took baby to baby spa
> Massage bath and oil

11 January

    I'm only human
    Never was a truer phrase
    Life is such a maze

12 January

    Vaccination day
    I'm sorry baby for that
    Wish I took the pain

13 January

    Induction at crèche
    Although it's not for a while
    Just want her to smile

14 January

    Three a.m. awake
    It's not you – baby, it's me
    Still struggle with health

15 January

    Yet more cancelled plans
    I've had enough of this now
    Caused another row

16 January

> Husband working more
> Hurts when he goes out the door
> Leaves me with the chores

17 January

> Today I am tired
> Tomorrow I will be too
> So worth it for you

18 January

> House hunting mayhem
> To dream big is to prepare –
> To fail or to thrive?

19 January

> Today could be worse
> But for sure could be better
> Struck myself with fridge!

20 January

> Inauguration
> Need I say anything more?
> New stories in store

21 January

>Poetry has caught
>The attention of masses
>Thank you Amanda

22 January

>Antwerp. Belgium. Here.
>Familiar yet trouble
>I'm so far away

23 January

>Lockdown blues have struck
>This mama got herself stuck
>Time for phone detox

24 January

>Feeling more like me
>After just one day phone-free
>Pressed reset – what glee!

25 January

>Reality check.
>Turned phone on: Full of drama
>But also new life

26 January

        Opportunity.
It knocks, it tempts, it calls me
      Should I stay or go?

27 January

      Every day is new
The world must seem so crazy
When you're five months old

28 January

      Another big spike
The home-sentence continues
    Covid – take a hike!

29 January

      Riots in Holland
Hooligans as protectors
    Saving their city

30 January

      It's funeral day
The dear father of a friend
  I watch the livestream

31 January

        The phrase of last year
   Now wins the human rights prize
       It's Black Lives Matter

Act 2

February

1 February

> Getting active now
> Five months post-partum fitness
> Female bodies: Wow

2 February

> The husband is sick
> Why do all men get man flu?
> I must do it all

3 February

> Excited so soon
> Six nations starts on weekend
> Wales to be in bloom!

4 February

> A lot going on
> Should I add some freelance work?
> Life's a marathon

5 February

> First day at day-care
> Feel both more and less like mum
> Emotions galore!

6 February
Not in a good place
Why does this keep happening?
Lockdown life is hard

7 February
Cried a lot today
Although my baby is great
Lockdown gave me hate

8 February
Today is brand new
The down patch I shall not stew
Don't want to feel blue

9 February
Not feeling myself
When not right physically,
The mental strain's real

10 February
Antibiotics
Twenty-four hours – what a change
No longer feel strange

11 February

> One-week day-care down
> I no longer have a frown
> My baby has grown

12 February

> Fair to say I'm up,
> And then equally I'm down
> The cycle repeats

13 February

> Away for weekend
> Should have been with my parents
> His parents instead

14 February

> Nature makes me smile
> Forget problems for a while
> Could walk and walk miles

15 February

> I post on social
> A jacuzzi pic of me
> Masks reality

16 February

I just love to write
Always had a book in me
Now it's poetry

17 February

Best friend is now bi
Got a girlfriend, not a guy
She is so happy!

18 February

Had hair cut at home
A huge change for all to see
Want to be "new me"

19 February

So much happening
Jesus the mum guilt is real!
Should not be big deal

20 February

Rugby has a sign
"Racism not accepted"
Sad that it's needed

21 February

    Six months old today
    Books are mainly for eating
    And she loves to play

22 February

    Filling at dentist!
    Breastfeeding can make teeth soft
    They don't tell you this!

23 February

    My baby girl's grown
    All the breastfeeding has shown
    Weight gaining nicely

24 February

    Good talk about sex
    We both want it more frisky
    That can be arranged!

25 February

    Appointment cancelled
    Sent me into a spiral
    Want to know what's wrong

26 February
>> Finally some news
>> Dermatologist was great
>> Have diagnosis

27 February
>> I now know what's wrong
>> But it comes as bittersweet
>> Breastfeeding must stop

28 February
>> I like. He doesn't.
>> House hunting – how to find one?
>> Will we ever move?

Act 3

March

1 March
> I start work this week
> Wish I wasn't feeling weak
> Health I need to seek

2 March
> I stopped breastfeeding
> Unimaginable pain
> Boobs are exploding

3 March
> Saw another house
> I know I am impatient
> Could this be the dream?

4 March
> First day back at work
> Did they do fine without me?
> Feeling all in doubt

5 March
> Am I doubting this?
> It is a win or a miss?
> Huge life decision

6 March

    Feeling insecure
    Is it three-sixty feedback?
    Or life decisions?

7 March

    The Pope's in Iraq
    Such a historic moment
    Extremism done?

8 March

    A second viewing
    This could be a game changer
    Are we doing this?

9 March

    Meghan and Harry
    Did interview with Oprah
    Bye-bye Piers Morgan!

10 March

    One year since lockdown
    Since I left the office life
    The struggle is rife

11 March
>
> Sarah Everard
> Shock waves through London and world
> Police has crisis

12 March
>
> Flutters and the shakes
> Struggle with anxiety
> But I shake it off

13 March
>
> Should we feel grateful
> For the times we made it home?
> It's men who must change

14 March
>
> My first mother's day
> Love you baby every way
> Not much else to say

15 March
>
> My husband is out
> Will he put an offer in?
> Heart is in my mouth

16 March

Sitting on the train
The commuter life is back!
Feel safe as ever

17 March

Sharing ideas
Copying is flattery
You think high of me

18 March

Husband is worried
What will make you happy though?
It's a good question

19 March

Don't know what to do
Worried about this and that
It's all-consuming

20 March

Negativity
Can't enjoy the finer things
What is wrong with me?

21 March

    Wales versus the French
    Beautiful game of rugby
    Fists are in a clench

22 March

    I'm struggling today
    But I would rather not say
    Keep it all at bay

23 March

    Do you get it though?
    To be down is to be blue
    Don't mean to blame you

24 March

    How can I express
    The way lockdown has made me?
    I am such a mess

25 March

    I need your support –
    'Til death do us part in short
    Give that food for thought

26 March

> We bought a new house!
> Now a move to the suburbs
> And a whole new life

27 March

> A walk and some wine
> Company has made us shine
> Life can be quite fine

28 March

> Nervous for the week
> Anxiety on Sundays
> Ruins the weekend

29 March

> You're my company
> Under trees writing with mum
> You inspire me

30 March

> It's amazing how
> The sun really changes me
> Can-do attitude

31 March

                Feel stressed to the max
            When will I be looked after?
                  Just want to relax

Act 4

April

1 April

    The life of a mum
    Do this, do that, look after
    When is it my turn?

2 April

    I get stressed at him
    Then stressed at the fucking cat
    Why does she do that?

3 April

    If I do nothing
    If I hide and go on strike
    Will he do it all?

4 April

    My daughter's asleep
    I'm trying it. I'm hiding
    Let's see what he does

5 April

    Let me tell you what
    Hiding out and striking works!
    Husband did a lot!

6 April

>Our place is for sale
>I'm nervous and I've gone pale
>Can't let plans derail

7 April

>Work life goes quite well
>Objectives galore but fun
>One by one they're done

8 April

>The pressure is on
>Even though I'm feeling strong
>Need to sell our home

9 April

>Prince Philip has died
>I feel sorry for the Queen
>A marriage so seen

10 April

>More deaths in the news
>Misunderstood TV star
>Anorexia

11 April

    Covid loneliness
    It is on my mind a lot
    She could have been saved

12 April

    Day-care closed for weeks
    Tried working with a baby?
    Can't take eyes off her

13 April

    It is a tough week
    But I handle stress better
    Keep getting stronger

14 April

    Plato said it first –
    "Discover people through play!"
    How I live my day

15 April

    I am new at this
    Still on this journey of "mum"
    But it's simply bliss

16 April

    Photos get the likes
   But stories make the money
     That is my motto

17 April

    Thinking about work
   Even though it's the weekend
    My mind goes berserk

18 April

     Back to baby spa
   Little girl almost eight months
    Where does the time go?

19 April

    I sit down to write
   Inspired by the greatest greats
    Tolstoy. Joyce. Dickens.

20 April

    To love is to read
   Lose yourself in other lands
    Fun is guaranteed

21 April

        Life is a story
    Your story is your asset
      Sell it to the world

22 April

        Anxiety strikes
  New mum still in pandemic
     It's normal I guess

23 April

    Called in for favour
  Get my "Selling Sunset" on
     Work renovations!

24 April

    My dreams are a weight
    To motivate just a few
     To write and create

25 April

     Life is cruel by far
 My heart breaks for you tonight
     The sky gained a star

26 April

>Pregnancy is tough
>A delight but also risk
>Sending luck to you!

27 April

>My relationship
>Grows. Strengthens. Diversifies.
>Every time I write.

28 April

>We must try to see
>To find the hope that exists
>No buts and no ifs

29 April

>Celeb lost a child
>Not a parent in the world
>Not thinking of you

30 April

>Impact at the time
>Is less than its later toll
>I'm not in my prime

Act 5
May

1 May

        Nice evening with friends
        But not the same as before
        When will take-out end?

2 May

        Our house isn't sold
        Feel my anxiety rise
        I need my allies

3 May

        Got my new tattoo
        A star that shines so brightly
        Stella – it's for you!

4 May

        People don't like change
        But then change becomes the norm
        Life can be a storm

5 May

        I am faking it
        Worried sick about all things
        But smiling on through

6 May

    Seem to be inspired
    When feeling sad or anxious
    Poetry's like this?

7 May

    Everyone dressed up
    We've been locked down for a year
    Wear those heels my dear!

8 May

    Guys I have a date
    A dinner with friends at eight
    Have to plan outfit

9 May

    Dinner out was great
    But I rush home to my girl
    I can't stay out late!

10 May

    It's not a mouth mask
    Dude – it's for your nose as well
    It's a simple task

11 May

> Some weeks you get no's
> No to every question
> But things always change!

12 May

> Sat in summer sun
> Now I feel like a writer
> This is so much fun

13 May

> All she sees is masks
> Odd year to be new in world
> Must be confusing

14 May

> I wear mine for you
> Show me the same courtesy
> Wear your mask for me

15 May

> Being in thirties
> What an interesting time
> A complex decade

16 May

    I'll be there for you
    I might forget a birthday
    But my love is true

17 May

    Could do with a break
    Wish my family could help
    It's a balance act

18 May

    The greatest news is
    When a friend has a baby
    His name is Jesse

19 May

    Do TV shows have
    An impact on your feelings?
    Think of what you watch

20 May

    The best compliment
    Told I have good energy
    Meant a lot to me

21 May

> You are nine months old
> Eight kilos and very long
> Where does the time go?

22 May

> The world is watching
> The situation is tense
> I pray for a truce

23 May

> Miserable May!
> Rained and rained and rained all day
> For what must we pay?

24 May

> I see you grow big
> Every day is something new
> Too good to be true

25 May

> My skin has cleared up!
> Now I can be real honest –
> Was a cancer scare

26 May

> I'm having these dreams –
> My husband keeps leaving me!
> Not reality!

27 May

> I had a week off
> I pressed reset on all things
> Now you hear me smile

28 May

> Everything will be
> Just the way it's planned to be
> Just you wait and see

29 May

> Big revelations!
> Out for dinner with my mum
> She's a naughty one!

30 May

> I am so content
> Nothing I would do to change
> We do complement

31 May

                He went and did it
           Got the job he so deserves!
             I am one proud wife!

Act 6

June

1 June

> Being self-aware
> Thinking about some coaching
> Better boss and wife!

2 June

> So much time has passed
> But now – FRIENDS reunion!
> The show that DID last

3 June

> Laughing with our friends
> They say we should have a show
> It's just how we are

4 June

> Watching TV shows
> Weird when their mood affects mine
> I get insecure

5 June

> Friendships are tricky
> 'Cause usually tied to guys
> Then they cut the ties

6 June

> More and more each day
> I am loving doing this
> Writing soothes my soul

7 June

> Happy when I write
> Can I do this every day?
> Love when work is play

8 June

> I am hurt by you
> True friends would not have done that
> I will walk away

9 June

> Friendships are complex
> Only gets harder with age
> Some last and some change

10 June

> Still think about friends
> All my best ones are so far
> Do I need some more?

11 June

> Almost two years late
> Practicing new signature
> 'Cause I took his name!

12 June

> Inspiration lives
> At times in the strangest place,
> Like in someone's eyes

13 June

> The moon is an arch
> Almost see that man sat there
> With his fishing rod

14 June

> Work was a struggle
> Conflicts and drama all round
> But solution found?

15 June

> The husband's birthday
> First one as a brand new dad
> Great times to be had

16 June

    Saw a fight in park
Is this just a primal thing?
    Don't understand men!

17 June

    Crazy as life gets
Remember not all is bad
    We are not there yet

18 June

    Body confidence
I feel good in my skin now
    Or maybe care less?

19 June

    Happy with my shape
Motherhood made me sexy
    It's all in the mind

20 June

    Always seek success
Put your mind to things you want
    Untangle the mess

21 June

>Pandemic effects –
>Cost of rural living soars
>Value of outdoors

22 June

>Endless washing piles
>Cannot reach "washbag zero"
>It's my highest goal

23 June

>The football is on –
>Drama and testosterone
>Clear I'm not a fan!

24 June

>In a coffee shop
>Hiding out to avoid him
>Hate it when we fight

25 June

>When a sad week hits
>You just know the good ones come
>Wait a bit longer

26 June

>Rushed to hospital!
>Turns out I had kidney stones
>So painful – but gone!

27 June

>If you saw me then
>Crawling out the house in pain
>But now back to me

28 June

>I can be Belgian!
>Application successful
>Now to speak pro Dutch

29 June

>Weird new weight loss tool
>Lets mouth open just a tad
>Surely this is bad

30 June

>Going to office
>I'm nervous about the change
>Is it 'cause I'm mum?

Act 7

July

1 July

    Tense conversations
    End of pandemic and work
    Not an easy fix

2 July

    Away for weekend
    Sometimes it just feels so good
    Sun, sea and good food

3 July

    Writing soothes my soul
    It's cliché but it's so true
    Best part of my day

4 July

    Take a deep breath in
    What weekends away are for
    Show that cheesy grin!

5 July

    Finding new balance
    I am shit-scared about it
    Being mum and boss

6 July

        Another work test
    Some people are hard to please
       Just do your damn best!

7 July

         Everyone has it
      So never stop creating
       We all have this gift

8 July

     She loves the ball pit
  Takes at least one everywhere
     At least there's plenty!

9 July

    She thinks she's a cat
  She crawled into litter box
    What to do 'bout that?

10 July

      It is moving day!
  Start of new suburban life
    First – all these boxes!

11 July

    Is it coming home?
    Watching the football final
    No – going to Rome!

12 July

    England should have won
    England had a lot at home
    It was theirs to lose

13 July

    I just want the best
    For me and my family
    I'll cope with the rest

14 July

    "It is what it is"
    Phrase my husband always says
    Can't change everything

15 July

    Our systems can't cope
    Third day of torrential rain
    Awful loss of life

16 July

> Devastating floods
> Climate change is very real
> Something must be done

17 July

> Lit a garden fire
> Hope the neighbours will not mind
> Lovely to feel free

18 July

> Staring at the flames
> My mind is empty but this
> Love the simple things

19 July

> Getting creative
> Coming up with new work plans
> I am excited

20 July

> Things can get too much
> Overworked and overtired
> I need a vacay!

21 July

> Don't take for granted
> The people who work with you
> Make them feel their best

22 July

> Have worked my ass off
> Trying to always excel
> Now I need a break

23 July

> The Olympic Games
> Has started and, no surprise –
> Covid cases rise

24 July

> Things have changed for sure
> People are nervous about
> All sorts of things now

25 July

> We start the planning
> Our little girl will turn one
> How the time has gone!

26 July

>No one is impressed
>If you send an email late
>Better to be good

27 July

>Instagram is odd
>They message like they are friends
>Where to draw the line?

28 July

>Our baby kisses
>all the other little ones
>Love is all she knows

29 July

>Off on holiday
>Driving to France 'cause we can
>Grateful to have this

30 July

>Holiday reading
>"Identity Crisis" is
>Food for thought for sure

31 July

   Coffee date with her
  The best date I could wish for
    My cute mini me

Act 8

August

1 August

    Writing sets me free
    Writing is my therapy
    My escape from life

2 August

    I realise now
    I don't have it bad at work
    Some friends really do

3 August

    Belarusian girl
    An Olympic athlete too
    So scared to go home

4 August

    Imminent crisis
    World is low on containers
    All shipping at risk

5 August

    Sold the apartment
    Things are coming together
    Huge relief for us

6 August

    Chose a new day-care
    Another piece of puzzle
    Slots into its place

7 August

    Sometimes feel alone
    I feel like they all gave up
    Don't care to visit

8 August

    Read books more slowly
    Is the latest health advice
    Better for the mind

9 August

    I still have worries
    Work and baby at day-care
    How will we manage?

10 August

    I know my problems
    Aren't the biggest or severe
    Must just persevere

11 August

        Work life kept apart
        I am a private person
        Don't want to share all

12 August

        World seems chaotic
        Praying for world peace seems like
        A childish pastime

13 August

        Friday the thirteenth
        Brought news of a shocking crime
        Quiet city mourns

14 August

        I take on so much
        A thousand projects at once
        Just need to decide

15 August

        Antwerp Mother's Day
        Had the best one full of play
        One to remember!

16 August

    Don't pass the stress on
When others are mean it's hard
    But you break the chain

17 August

    Never start email
"I am disappointed that…"
  It does not feel good!

18 August

   Feedback is a gift
But you have to be careful
 Can come across cruel

19 August

  As the saying goes
"I am still an embryo"
 I have still to grow

20 August

 Don't send angry mails
Think it through – would you like it?
  We should all be kind

21 August

My baby is one!
Wow that year went by so fast
It was so much fun

22 August

Surrounded by friends
It feels so good to gather
Even if outside

23 August

"Your password is weak"
But so is my memory!
Need to keep this one

24 August

Had the best date night
Working out plans for a change
New life to adjust

25 August

I had a sex dream!
It wasn't my husband though
Why was HE in it?

26 August

> Hard to say goodbye
> Never quite sure of next time
> I will miss you mum

27 August

> I'm a cry baby
> Everything sets me off now
> Since I became mum

28 August

> I overthink things
> Not sure why I dream these things
> Things are mad it seems

29 August

> Need to watch 'Sex/Life'
> Apparently I'll relate
> But that seems extreme

30 August

> All of us matter
> People are more than numbers
> Let's remember that

31 August

        A friend is someone
    You may not have seen in years
       Show up when in need

Act 9

September

1 September

        Inner peace on news
      Something we all need at work
         But how to get there?

2 September

        Working so damn hard
       Grafting like a crazy loon
        Project will succeed!

3 September

          I think I inspired
    My best friend wants to write now
        Just three lines a day

4 September

         I am proud of her
    Changed her life in just two months
        We're not who we were

5 September

        Feeling super sick
      Have to keep it together
       Mums get no days off

6 September
>Three-year-old rescued
>Found after three days in wild
>I'm in floods of tears!

7 September
>Fight with the husband
>Usually we're such a team
>But now being mean

8 September
>I put my all in
>But have commute and baby -
>Feel guilty all round

9 September
>A record commute
>Almost four hours door to door
>Imagine my mood!

10 September
>Had the best advice
>Good enough is good enough
>Needed to hear it

11 September

    Sometimes the advice
    Comes from those we least expect
    So be receptive

12 September

    There are no "pop" songs
    About politics or law
    It's not glam enough

13 September

    Saying a prayer
    Friend's babies in hospital
    Praying for the best

14 September

    Anniversary
    Means always and forever
    I'm in your corner

15 September

    We are all human
    He forgot his work laptop
    We work around it!

16 September

>Commuters' lesson
>Late trains only get later
>They won't make up time

17 September

>It's times like this that
>Make you realise what is
>Important in life

18 September

>Unleashed butterflies
>The feeling you give me babe
>When you look at me

19 September

>No me without you
>Appreciation moment
>I love you husband

20 September

>Friendship groups are weird
>Groups within groups within groups
>Sometimes feel left out

21 September
          What an odd birthday
          Highs and lows and health concerns
          Cousin must pull through!

22 September
          I try to like her
          You know when you try, but can't?
          Smile, roll eyes and nod

23 September
          Cousin doing fine
          Still has many tests to go
          Have our fingers crossed

24 September
          "I do not see race"
          Is an ignorant comment
          Have to know to grow

25 September
          She is growing up
          Even has her own friends now
          Still my little pup!

26 September
>
> Can we clarify
> Living abroad is hard work
> Even though it's fun

27 September
>
> Feeling positive
> Started five minute journal
> Choose to be happy

28 September
>
> Do I miss climbing?
> Miss friends more than sport itself
> Was my social life

29 September
>
> I saw a life coach
> This will help me grow in my
> Profession and life

30 September
>
> We seem to go through
> The same things at the same time
> Why we are best friends

Act 10

October

1 October

        Making New Year plans
        Will introduce my daughter
        To some of my friends

2 October

        Things are scarier
        In the cover of darkness
        Even walking round

3 October

        I get nervous when
        Feeling I'm the only one
        Awake at this hour

4 October

        Believe in hard work
        Manifest on what you want
        I am a writer

5 October

        Feeling sad today
        Disconnected from it all
        Overwhelmed by life

6 October
　　　　I can trust others
　Team work does make the dream work
　　　　Slowly learning this

7 October
　　　　God I love that rush
　　The surge of take-off power
　　　　Love my work travel

8 October
　　　　I just feel so free
　　When soaring above the world
　　　　Love being on planes

9 October
　　　　Barriers for "her"
　　The elephant in the room
　　　　You should just say hi

10 October
　　　　Women must support
　　Each other in this tough world
　　　　Fix each other's crowns

11 October
> I feel so needed
> So blessed I call you my friend
> Be there 'til the end

12 October
> Parents have covid!
> Picked it up from my sister
> Looked after her kids

13 October
> Parents are not well
> Irresponsible of her
> To ask mum to come

14 October
> Why is it so hard
> To walk not run down the stairs?
> I do this weird dance!

15 October
> Another MP
> Doing his daily duty
> Had his life cut short

16 October

        I was an odd child
        'Peculiar' was my name
        Will she be the same?

17 October

        Parents picking up
        Still not over this yet though
        Even with vaccine

18 October

        Took the day off work
        Mostly organising things
        Would men do this too?

19 October

        Train platform is still
        Not a sound but then that guy
        Let out a huge fart!

20 October

        How to delegate?
        Realise it's such a skill
        A skill! Not lazy

21 October

    I fear the future
This generation of "more"
    Could ruin it all

22 October

    Working parent life
Whose meeting is more crucial?
    Other picks up child

23 October

    Can you imagine
What it's like to recognise
    Your name the first time?

24 October

    Stuck on this subject!
My daughter hears "Stella!" yelled
    She thinks – "Oh, that's me!"

25 October

    It is a sad day
News that Gunther from Friends died
    TV will miss him

26 October

    Had a fight with sis
Then her husband starts to call
    This is not normal?

27 October

    Trying my best here
Only just holding my shit
  Don't need yours on top

28 October

   Balance is real hard
Feel pushed in all directions
   Have to be selfish

29 October

    Not natural me
But only here for two days
  Try to people please

30 October

  Wedding day of friend
Spooky Halloween weekend
The witch just got hitched!

31 October

        Weekends are so short
        But how wonderful to see
        Friends and family

Act 11

November

1 November
>She is dramatic
>My diplomacy dyke groans
>Hard relationship

2 November
>Anxiety rise
>You feel it seep up your chest
>And your heart's pounding

3 November
>When your heart beats fast
>Find what works for you to cope
>For me, I just breathe

4 November
>Need good influence
>Sorry – I can't add drama
>Need to self-protect

5 November
>Totally confused
>What am I supposed to be?
>A mum or a boss?

6 November

        Don't try to fool me
    You can run and you can hide
       I see through disguise

7 November

      The cat went missing!
    Gave us both such a panic
      Now he is grounded

8 November

     Face masks only stress
  The importance of kind eyes
      Eyes can say a lot

9 November

      Negative feedback
  But always productive ways
    To say things you say

10 November

     Lonely as a mum
  And lonely as a boss too
    What you gonna do?

11 November

> Off on holiday!
> Feels like first moment of year
> I get to relax

12 November

> All-inclusive stays
> Give me a slight discomfort
> Gluttony is real

13 November

> Inspiration lies
> In everything around you
> Pay close attention

14 November

> Holiday date night
> And I cried for an hour straight!
> Talking about stress

15 November

> Lose myself in books
> Power of escapism
> All for stress-free life

16 November

        The thing with sex is
The more had the more you want
        Addictive substance

17 November

        What a nice relax
    Holiday with all parents
        All get on so well

18 November

      Not going home yet
Rebooked flight to stay longer
      We have no regrets!

19 November

       Sailing in the sun
Feel wind and sea in my hair
       Forget any woes

20 November

       Sun and family
   Definition of relaxed
    Lucky with this love

21 November

    I have missed the sun
    The way it feels on my skin
    Blessed, healthy, sun-kissed

22 November

    You had a baby
    She will enter your dreams soon
    A crazy moment

23 November

    We are lucky ones
    So much love in family
    Even parents gel!

24 November

    She has such kind eyes
    Reassures me with one look
    All will be okay

25 November

    I question so much
    I know it's not good for me
    Confidence is key

26 November

    We all have a gift
    We are all meant to create
    Manifest talent

27 November

    In a silly mood
    So all my contacts get memes
    Don't worry – not rude!

28 November

    I feel stronger now
    Okay with our timetable
    Do life at our pace

29 November

    This pandemic sucks
    Let's be real for a second
    What wave are we now?

30 November

    She is so funny
    Only she could have stories
    Of fun in crisis

Act 12

December

1 December
>
> No one responded
> Just noticed now that it seems
> No one liked the memes!

2 December
>
> A book shop with wine
> All these authors inspire me
> Manifesting this!

3 December
>
> My mind still fragile
> Realise this more and more
> Careful what I watch!

4 December
>
> Heart-breaking story
> Six-year old could not trust those
> Who should protect him

5 December
>
> Happy eyes sparkle
> Do you know how loved you are?
> All you know is love

6 December

    "All you know is love"
    Made this into little song
    She just nods along

7 December

    Trusted cat-sitter
    But I went and lost the keys!
    I found them, thank God!

8 December

    Just realised now
    Never told her I lost keys
    Guess she might know now?

9 December

    My mum broke her toe!
    Ask how? She dropped a breadboard!
    She needs to relax

10 December

    Had day of mum guilt
    Felt guilt about feeling guilt!
    Mad rollercoaster!

11 December
>
> In Rome for work trip
> Feels odd to be on the road
> Rome makes my heart skip

12 December
>
> Always feels so good
> To come home to family
> See that little face

13 December
>
> Eddie Redmayne wows
> In a blinder of a show
> Can't wait to watch it!

14 December
>
> Tornado in States
> I can't imagine the fear
> And this time of year

15 December
>
> Social media
> Things you say can resurface
> So write with purpose

16 December
        Love you to the moon
        Sometimes you drive me crazy
        But you are my goon

17 December
        Finished work for year
        And even got my booster
        Ready for a break

18 December
        Finished work on high
        Even for all ups and downs
        I do enjoy work

19 December
        Panic about trip!
        French government changed the rules
        Hope we still make it

20 December
        UK has shortage
        Of lateral flow tests now
        There's always something

21 December

>Recently informed
>About real postpartum rage
>Want to help these mums

22 December

>That smile on my face
>I'm the cat that got the cream
>We are together

23 December

>Seeing family
>We introduce our baby
>She is sixteen months

24 December

>Our poor little babe
>Car sick on a country drive
>Breaks my heart each time

25 December

>It is Christmas Day!
>Everywhere I look are smiles
>The trip was worth it

26 December

> Boxing Day curry
> It's a tradition I guess
> We eat in excess!

27 December

> Almost end of year
> Will next year be forgiving?
> We all need a break

28 December

> Elizabeth Holmes
> Deliberation takes days
> Will they convict her?

29 December

> The hoops we go through
> Don't really know what to do
> For us to get home

30 December

> Amount of money
> Spent on needless covid tests
> Really grinds my gears

31 December
>
> End of whirlwind year
> Is the time right? Is it now?
> Try for baby two...